To my parents, for encouraging me to write.
To our living planet, for the inspiration of what to write about.

—SMB

To Lottie — soar high and fly.

—JL

Text Copyright © 2019 Sheri Mabry Bestor
Illustration Copyright © 2019 Jonny Lambert
Design Copyright © 2019 Sleeping Bear Press

Content Expert: Lynn Kimsey, Professor of Entomology, University of California, Davis

Sleeping Bear Press

2395 South Huron Parkway, Suite 200
Ann Arbor, MI 48104
www.sleepingbearpress.com

Printed and bound in the United States.

10 9 8 7 6 5 4 3 2

Library of Congress Cataloging-in-Publication Data

Names: Bestor, Sheri Mabry, author. | Lambert, Jonny, illustrator.
Title: Soar high, dragonfly! / written by Sheri Mabry Bestor ; illustrated by
 Jonny Lambert.
Description: Ann Arbor, MI : Sleeping Bear Press, [2019] | Audience: Age 4-8.
Identifiers: LCCN 2018037511 | ISBN 9781585364107 (hardcover)
Subjects: LCSH: Dragonflies—Juvenile literature. | Dragonflies—Life
 cycles—Juvenile literature.
Classification: LCC QL520 .B49 2019 | DDC 595.7/33—dc23
LC record available at https://lccn.loc.gov/2018037511

Soar High, Dragonfly!

By Sheri Mabry Bestor and Illustrated by Jonny Lambert

Spring sun warms the earth. Seeds sprout. Birds build nests.

High above, tiny wings hum like wind through the leaves.

The green darner dragonfly is one of several dragonfly species that migrate. That means that the dragonflies travel long distances, sometimes across the country and even into another country, to find a new place to live. The adult green darner's wings are translucent (clear enough to let light through) and sometimes have a tint of color.

The female dragonflies are ready to lay their eggs.

One lands on the surface of a pond.

Another, perches on a water plant.

Pop.

Pop.

Pop.

Some dragonflies insert their eggs into the stem of a plant to help protect the baby insects. Others lay their eggs directly in the water.

Tiny eggs are tucked inside a stem. They are safe, waiting to hatch.

Rains come.

Drip.

The pond fills.

Drip.

Drop.

Drip.

Drop.

Drop.

The stem is covered with water.

The eggs seep into the pond. For many days, the eggs float on the water's surface. Some are eaten. Some are washed away.

Dragonfly eggs are very small and have no way to protect themselves. Many are eaten by fish, frogs, and other insects before they have a chance to hatch.

And some... hatch.

Out swims a nymph!

Oh my, a baby dragonfly!

Baby dragonflies are called nymphs. Do you think that the nymph looks like a dragonfly? Not really, right? That's because a dragonfly goes through incomplete metamorphosis, which means that it has three stages: egg, nymph, and adult. The nymphs go through several changes before they become an adult.

The nymph is hungry. He spots food. He squirts water out behind him so he can move forward. He thrusts out his tiny jaw and captures his prey with one scoop.

Gulp!

Nymphs squirt water out of their back ends to propel themselves forward. This movement helps them capture food. They are predators, so they eat other living things in the water.

He swims and eats and swims and eats.

As he eats, he grows. As he grows, he sheds his casing.

Squirt. Gulp!

Squirt. Gulp!

Nymphs have an outer casing, and when the inside of their body grows too big, they need to shed the outer casing and grow a new one that fits better. This process, called molting, happens several times, until the nymph is ready for the final shedding.

Days fade into nights. Nights open into days. The nymph is ready.

He waits until it is dark and safe.

He climbs, crawling up

up

up onto a reed. Out of the water, finally.

Crawl high, dragonfly!

Do you think this looks like a dragonfly now? When new dragonflies first emerge, they are wet and their wings are folded tight—they aren't ready for flight yet.

His final casing has grown too tight. It cracks. He wiggles and squiggles. Out he crawls! His wings are free at last! But the new dragonfly is too tired to fly.

When the sun peeks up, the dragonfly's wings dry in its warmth. They hum in the morning light. He stretches and straightens. He adjusts his wings to the slant of the breeze. He uses his thorax to launch himself…

and…

he's flying!

Soar high, dragonfly!

When a new dragonfly emerges from the water and molts for the final time, his wings are wet and have not unfurled yet. He can't fly, which makes him easy prey for a predator. When the dragonfly stretches and pumps his wings, they begin to dry and soon he is ready for flight!

Although he has never flown before, he is an expert. He can fly forward. He can fly backward. He can fly fast. He can even hover in midair.

Dragonflies are expert fliers and can travel very fast through the air. Some scientists study dragonflies' flying techniques to help with the designs of aircraft.

His large eyes wrap around his head, so he can scan every direction at the same time. He spots a bird coming at him!

Uh-oh!

He darts! And gets away.

Each eye of this dragonfly has 25 lenses and can rotate almost 360 degrees, making the dragonfly skilled at seeing prey and predators.

The dragonfly catches insects as he flies.
One after another, clearing the sky.

Catch! Grab! Snatch!

Dragonflies eat mosquitoes. Many people welcome the sight of
a sky filled with dragonflies on warm, buggy summer evenings.

Oops!

Missed one.

Good try, dragonfly!

The sun begins to sink. The air cools. To stay warm, the dragonfly lands on a leaf and tips his wings to catch the fading sun.

Dragonflies have special ways to keep warm. They can capture the heat of the sun by adjusting their four wings just right.

When darkness falls, his body changes color.

Oh my, dragonfly!

Some male dragonflies turn purple when they are cool. This helps them to absorb the heat.

Dragonflies cling under vegetation during hard rains.
But, in a lighter rain, the nanostructure of the dragonfly's
wings allows water to roll off, taking dust and dirt with it.

Morning breaks, and so does a rainstorm!
Heavy droplets shower down. The dragonfly
finds his way under a leaf and clings there.

Stay dry, dragonfly!

When the skies have cleared, the dragonfly finds a mate. Together, they fly through the sky like a letter O floating on the wind.

Dragonflies that are mating hold on to each other as they fly through the air. When they are ready, they separate, and the female will lay eggs. The male sometimes hovers nearby to protect the female.

Autumn cools the air. Leaves burst into color. High above, tiny wings hum like wind through the leaves. It's time for the dragonflies to go. To find warmer days. To lay their eggs. And to start again.

Bye-bye, dragonfly!

Young dragonflies have an instinct to migrate and find a warmer climate where they can lay eggs and begin the life cycle all over again.